OWLS

HUNTERS OF THE NIGHT

Elaine Landau

WORDS TO KNOW

binocular vision—The ability to focus both eyes on an object at once.

burrow—A tunnel or hole in the ground used by an animal.

camouflage—The use of an animal's coloring to blend in with surroundings.

mate—The process through which animals have young. A mate can also be the female or male partner of an animal.

nocturnal—Active at night.

predator—An animal that kills other animals for food.

prey—An animal that is hunted for food.

raptor—A bird with strong legs, powerful feet, and sharp claws.

species—A type of animal.

talons—Razor-sharp claws.

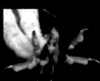

CONTENTS

A BIRD OF THE NIGHT

A large owl sits quietly in a tree after dark. The strong bird seems to be resting. Yet this owl is awake and hungry.

Suddenly, it flies from the tree. Seconds later, it grabs a mouse with its strong, sharp claws. Carrying the small animal in its beak, the owl flies away.

Most owls are nocturnal birds. They are active at night while you are asleep. That is why you rarely see them. Yet owls are amazing creatures. If you would like to know more about them—read on.

A barn owl lands on a tree stump.

INTRODUCING THE OWL

There are many different species of owls. Some are quite large while others are very small. A great gray owl can grow as tall as 33 inches. Its wings measure about 60 inches across. That is about the length of a bathtub.

The elf owl is very small. It grows no more than 5 to 6 inches tall. That is just a little shorter than a new pencil.

There are lots of other owls in between these. Some weigh as little as one and a half ounces and others as much as nine pounds. The great horned owl is a large, heavy owl. Barn owls are medium-sized owls. The Northern Saw-whet owl has a small body with a large head.

A great gray owl

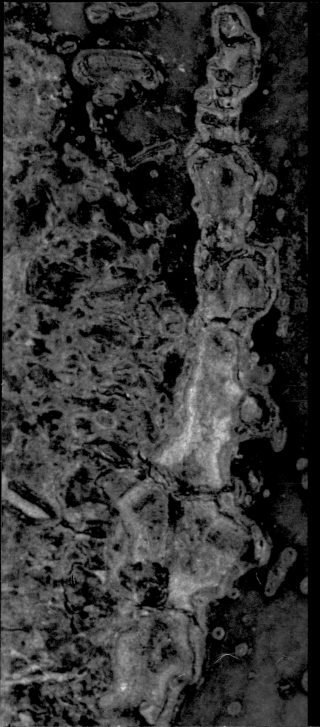

Though owls are birds, they are the same as humans in some ways. They sit upright. Owls also have eyes in the same place as those of people. Owls look straight ahead. They seem to stare at you. Most other birds have eyes on the sides of their heads.

Different owls have different calls. Not all sound like they are saying "whoo" or "hoot." Some owls make a barking sound. Others hiss, whistle, snort, or screech. The barred owl's call sounds like "Who cooks for you?"

Unlike other birds, owls have eyes on the front of their heads. This elf owl looks out from a tree.

9

The Owl's History and Mystery

Owls were here before people. Scientists have found owl fossils that date back to dinosaur days. Drawings of owls have also been found in caves. Some of these drawings are over eighteen thousand years old.

Some people believe owls are wise or have special abilities. Today you see them on Halloween cards and in Harry Potter movies, doing things owls cannot really do.

Owls do not have magic powers. They are simply birds living in the wild.

This metal statue of an owl was made in South America about two thousand years ago.

READY FOR NIGHT LIFE

The soft tips of this eastern screech owl's wings help it fly silently through the night.

Most owls are night birds. Their senses help them survive in the dark.

Owls pick up sounds that people cannot hear. This helps them hunt the animals they eat after dark. An owl can hear a mouse running in the leaves over twenty yards away.

Most owls can also see well even in dim light. Unlike most birds, owls have binocular vision. They can focus both eyes on an object at once. This helps them see how near their prey is. Some people think that owls can turn their heads completely around, but this is not so.

Not only do many animals not see owls at night, they also do not hear them. Owls have feathers with soft tips. Birds with feathers that have hard tips make a swooshing sound in flight. But an owl's prey will not hear the owl coming because of its feathers' soft tips.

HUNTING AND EATING

Owls eat many different kinds of food. The largest owls hunt hares, squirrels, young foxes, large birds, and other animals. Smaller owls live mostly on insects, frogs, lizards, and mice. Some types of Asian and African owls eat fish.

Owls are raptors. These are birds that eat other animals. All raptors have extremely strong legs and powerful feet. Owls also have razor-sharp claws called talons.

This tawny owl carries a mouse in its beak. The owl will feed its babies with the mouse.

A great horned owl
in Arizona makes
its nest in a cactus.

The talons are used to grasp and kill prey. Some owls use their large hooked beaks to help with this. Owls often also use their talons to carry their prey through the air.

Owls do not chew their food. Small prey is swallowed whole. Owls use their beaks and talons to tear up larger prey. These pieces are swallowed without chewing as well.

The prey's bones, teeth, claws and feathers are coughed up in small, hard balls, called pell Scientists and students som study these pellets to learn mo about what owls eat.

16

WHERE THE OWLS ARE

Owls live on every continent but Antarctica. Owls can be found in very cold places as well as in hot deserts. Many live in forests or wooded areas. Owls are also found on farmlands and grasslands.

Not all owls nest in trees. Burrowing owls nest underground. They use the old burrows of ground squirrels, prairie dogs, and other small animals.

Most owls tend to stay far away from humans. But barn owls and screech owls sometimes live in barns, church steeples, and other buildings. These owls feed on mice and rats near farms and towns.

OWL ENEMIES

Larger adult owls have few **predators**, or animals that eat them. But, when they are young, they are in more danger. About half of all owl chicks do not grow into adults. Other animals eat them while they are young.

Smaller owls have many enemies. Larger owls, coyotes, weasels, hawks, raccoons, and other animals eat them. An owl's coloring often helps hide it. This is known as **camouflage**.

Some owls' brown and gray feathers blend in well with tree bark. It is hard to spot one roosting in a tree. Saw-whet owls roost in the densest part of trees. Predators cannot easily see them there. The mostly white snowy owl lives in open areas as far north as the Arctic. Its white feathers make it hard to spot as well.

The snowy owl blends in
well with its snowy home.

HAVING BABIES

Owls mate and have babies. Some owls keep the same mate for life. Other types have many different mates.

Owls lay their eggs in a nest. But they usually do not build their own nests. Instead, owls often use nests left by other birds.

Most female owls lay between two and six eggs. These eggs will hatch in fifteen to thirty-five days. The owl chicks are not all born at once. They usually hatch about two days apart.

A male and female tawny owl roost together in a tree.

RAISING YOUNG

Young owl chicks are helpless. They are blind at birth and have only a thin layer of down, or feathers, for warmth. They need their mother's care to stay alive.

The mother owl feeds her chicks and protects them from predators. Father owls bring back food for the family, too. At first, the chicks eat insects. As they grow older, they have larger prey.

The chicks learn to hunt and fly while with their parents. After about two or three months, they are ready to leave the nest.

Baby screech owls have fluffier feathers than their parents.

OWLS AND PEOPLE

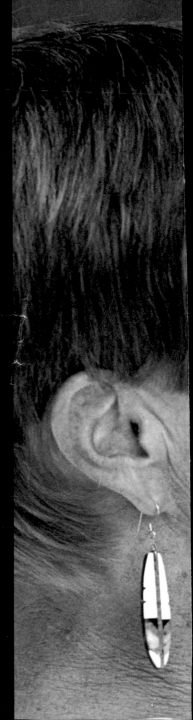

Owls are helpful to humans. They eat mice and insects that harm farm crops. Yet many owl species are in trouble. They are sometimes poisoned when farm fields are sprayed with chemicals to kill weeds and insects. Hunting owls is against the law in the United States. But these birds are sometimes hunted anyway.

Owls need wide-open spaces and forests to live. But in a lot of areas, such places are disappearing. Many trees have been cut down for timber. Wooded areas are also often cleared to build houses.

Such areas are also home to the owl's prey. When these areas are gone, owls lose the food they need.

Dr. Kathleen Ramsey takes care of a Mexican spotted owl. Ramsey works at the wildlife center near Espanola, New Mexico.

THE FUTURE

With our help, owls can have a better future. Laws have been passed to protect these birds from being hunted or poisoned.

In some places, laws also protect the owl's home area, which is known as its habitat. This is very important. Some owls are endangered. This means they are at risk of dying out.

We need to make sure that owls are here in the future. It is up to humans to protect them.

A burrowing owl sits near a sign for a protected bird-nesting area.

BIRD NESTING AREA

KEEP OUT

BIRD NESTING AREAS ARE PROTECTED BY STATE AND FEDERAL LAW. DO NOT ENTER THIS AREA BETWEEN

JAN.- and JUNE.-

(Date) _(Date)_

NOTICE: THE AREA BEHIND THIS SIGN IS AN IMPORTANT BIRD NESTING SITE. DISTURBANCE BY HUMANS OR PETS CAN CAUSE NEST ABANDONMENT AND DEATH OF YOUNG BIRDS.

Florida Game & Fresh Water Fish Commission

FUN FACTS ABOUT OWLS

★ Female owls are usually bigger than males. Some scientists think they are bigger so they can protect the nest. Others believe that females need to catch larger prey than males.

★ An owl has a lot of feathers on its legs and feet. This is to protect it from snake and rat bites.

★ Owls are not the "wisest" birds. Parrots as well as some other birds are smarter.

★ It is illegal to own an owl as a pet in the United States.

★ Owl mummies have been found in the tombs of ancient Egyptian rulers.

★ Barn owls are better at catching mice than cats are. A family of barn owls will eat about thirteen hundred mice a year.

★ Barn owls are sometimes called "monkey-faced owls" because of their white heart-shaped faces and dark eyes.

Some people think barn owls' faces look like those of monkeys.

TO KNOW MORE ABOUT OWLS

BOOKS

Gibbons, Gail. *Owls*. New York: Holiday House, 2005.

Lynch, Wayne. *Owls*. Minnetonka, Minn.: NorthWind Press, 2005.

Markle, Sandra. *Owls*. Minneapolis: Carolrhoda Books, 2004.

Murray, Julie. *Owls*. Edina, Minn.: ABDO Publishing Co., 2005.

Riley, Joelle. *Quiet Owls*. Minneapolis: Lerner, 2004.

INTERNET ADDRESSES

Lake Milton Raptor Education Center

Visit this home for wild birds of prey. Do not miss the photo gallery for some great pictures of owls and other raptors.

<http://www.raptorcenter.org>

World Owl Trust

This group is working to see that all owl species in the world survive.

<http://www.owls.org>

INDEX

Enslow Elementary, an imprint of Enslow Publishers, Inc.

Enslow Elementary® is a registered trademark of Enslow Publishers, Inc.

Library of Congress Cataloging-in-Publication Data

Landau, Elaine.
    Owls : hunters of the night / Elaine Landau.
        p. cm. — (Animals after dark)
    Includes bibliographical references and index.
    ISBN-13: 978-0-7660-2768-8
    ISBN-10: 0-7660-2768-6
    1. Owls—Juvenile literature. I. Title. II. Series.
QL696.S8L26 2006
598.9'7—dc22   2006014966

Printed in the United States of America

10 9 8 7 6 5 4 3 2 1

To Our Readers: We have done our best to make sure all Internet Addresses in this book were active and appropriate when we went to press. However, the author and the publisher have no control over and assume no liability for the material available on those Internet sites or on other Web sites they may link to. Any comments or suggestions can be sent by e-mail to comments@enslow.com or to the address on the back cover.

Series Literacy Advisor: Dr. Allan A. De Fina, Department of Literacy Education, New Jersey City University.

Illustration Credits: © 2003-2006 Shutterstock, Inc., p. 29; © 2006 Jupiterimages Corporation, pp. 2 (bottom left and bottom right), 4–5, 22–23, 28, 32; © AP/Wide World Photos, pp. 24–25; © Bailey, Linda/Animals Animals–Earth Scenes, pp. 26–27; © Corel Corporation, pp. 2 (top left and top right), 3, 6–7; © MCDONALD, JOE/Animals Animals–Earth Scenes, pp. 12–13; © Nathan Benn/Corbis, pp. 10–11; © NHPA/Ernie Janes, pp. 20–21; © Rick and Nora Bowers/Visuals Unlimited, pp. 1, 8–9, 16–17; © Stephen Dalton/Minden Pictures, pp. 14–15; © Tom Mangelsen/naturpl.com, pp. 18–19.

Cover Illustration: © Rick and Nora Bowers/Visuals Unlimited.

Enslow Elementary
an imprint of

Enslow Publishers, Inc.
40 Industrial Road
Box 398
Berkeley Heights, NJ 07922
USA

http://www.enslow.com